WHERE LEADERSHIP BEGINS.

JOURNAL

Where Leadership Begins - Journal

Concept: Dan Freschi

Cover Design, Interior Graphics: Claire E. Weber

Interior Layout: Griffin Mill

ISBN: 978-1-957351-31-5

Published by Nico 11 Publishing & Design,
Mukwonago, Wisconsin
Michael Nicloy, Publisher
www.nico11publishing.com

Quantity and wholesale order requests can be emailed to:
mike@nico11publishing.com
or can be made by phone: 217.779.9677

Be well read.

Printed in The United States of America

In case of loss, please return to:

____

____

____

____

____

THIS IS <u>YOUR</u> JOURNAL

"Everything starts with the individual because all meaningful change comes from the inside-out. Systematic organizational change can't happen without changes in individual behavior."
– Dr. Stephen R. Covey

Hi! I am so glad you are here.

In your hands is a companion journal to *Where Leadership Begins*. Use this to effectively evaluate where leadership begins for you. These pages are where you can sort through the activities in the book and appendices, and take time to reflect on the choices you've made to get you where you are today.

Use this journal to evaluate and reflect on:

- The choices that are informed by a deep understanding of how you see yourself and how others see you.
- The choices that are true to who you are as a leader and a person.
- The choices that seek to elevate others instead of yourself.
- The choices that pursue the best outcome even if they open you up to doubt or ridicule.
- The choices that are grounded in courage instead of fear.

As a leader, carving out time for daily journaling is a significant choice. It not only fosters personal growth, but it can also catalyze inspiring your team through the act of thoughtful leadership.

Journaling offers a unique opportunity to explore and evaluate your thoughts, ideas, and challenges in an organized and constructive manner.

When journaling is done consistently, it can lead to a greater understanding of your choices, what you're experiencing, your strengths, areas for development, and steps to take for leadership excellence. It provides a safe and non-judgmental space to express your emotions, concerns, and reflections on your daily life, leadership choices, and experiences. When you journal, you encourage self-awareness and vulnerability, which are essential for personal growth and understanding your authentic self as a leader.

Dedicating time to examine your choice, values, experiences, emotions, and leadership style will provide invaluable insights into your leadership growth. Embrace your vulnerability and authenticity in these reflections, which can be a powerful catalyst for change and improvement.

Journaling as a leader is an enriching experience when approached with an open and optimistic mindset. Your journal can become a treasure trove of inspiration, a space where self-awareness, authenticity, humility, vulnerability, and courage converge. And maybe one day you will be inspired to write your own book.

As you develop your journaling habit, I wanted to again share the five choices that are detailed in *Where Leadership Begins*:

Choosing to be self-aware. We all have strengths and weaknesses, parts of ourselves we like and parts we would prefer to stay hidden. There are even parts of ourselves we aren't aware of but others would instantly recognize. Choosing to become a leader starts with making a conscious choice to explore all aspects of ourselves and how they affect our personal and professional relationships.

Choosing to be authentic. Can you be a leader and have self-doubts? Can you make a mistake? Can you admit to not having the answer? When you choose to be authentic, you're willing to risk infallibility for something much more relatable and inspiring – being human.

Choosing to be humble. Humility seems to fly in the face of what today's leadership demands. Leaders are depicted in the media as unflappable, always thinking three steps ahead, always able to adapt to the unexpected. In real life, leadership begins with actual human relationships and an understanding that they are a small but essential part of a greater objective.

Choosing to be vulnerable. Much like humility, we don't often attribute vulnerability as a hallmark of good leadership. But if you seek to get the best out of those you lead and interact with, you need to break down the walls you or your organization constructs between leader and led. In many team sports, you'll hear of a "player's coach," one the players will "run through a brick wall for." That special kind of relationship begins with vulnerability.

Choosing to be courageous. Underpinning all of these attributes – and so many others – is courage. I'm not talking about the courage to make a hard decision or address a large crowd, although these things are often required of leaders. But the courage to be yourself, to admit your flaws, to be willing to share your true self with those who rely on you for their livelihoods as well as those who have a more traditional view of leadership. Trust me, it's easier to play it safe – but that also can introduce its own problems and limit your effectiveness as a leader.

I wish you the best on your leadership journey. Let me know how it's going. I'd love to hear from you.

www.ingramcontent.com/pod-product-compliance
Lightning Source LLC
Chambersburg PA
CBHW071554210326
41597CB00019B/3245
* 9 7 8 1 9 5 7 3 5 1 3 1 5 *